A STORY ABOUT CANCER

(WITH A HAPPY ENDING)

India Desjardins

Marianne Ferrer

A STORY ABOUT
CANCER
(WITH A HAPPY ENDING)

India Desjardins

Marianne Ferrer

Translated by Solange Ouellet

Frances Lincoln
Children's Books

The colours on the walls, floor and ceiling all melt together as I slowly make my way down the hospital corridor. In just a few minutes, they're going to tell me how much time I have left to live.

Pale blue, pale green, pale pink, beige...

Whoever decided on the colour scheme in this hospital
must have failed their final exam in interior design.

They've even redecorated in the five
years that I've been coming here, but I
can never find anything that's changed.
It just seems newer and cleaner.

With the same awful colours.

Annie, my favourite nurse, told me they chose these colours because they're supposed to calm you down.

Honestly, I can't imagine anyone coming here and getting hyper after the kind of treatments you get.

Do colours really change anything? I don't know...

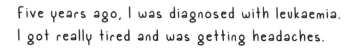

Five years ago, I was diagnosed with leukaemia.
I got really tired and was getting headaches.

They sent me for all kinds of tests.

I was only ten years old and I'd never heard of anyone who had this disease. I didn't know exactly what it was and I don't think we ever talked about cancer in my family before that.

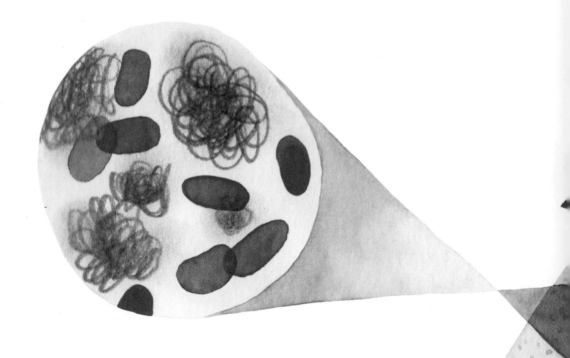

If I heard anyone talking about it I probably just ignored them and carried on thinking about other things. I was obsessed with a boy band at the time, and I won't even mention the name because it's too embarrassing to think about it now.

The smell of the hospital seeps in all around me. It doesn't smell good, but it's not that bad, either. It's a mix of disinfectant and illness.

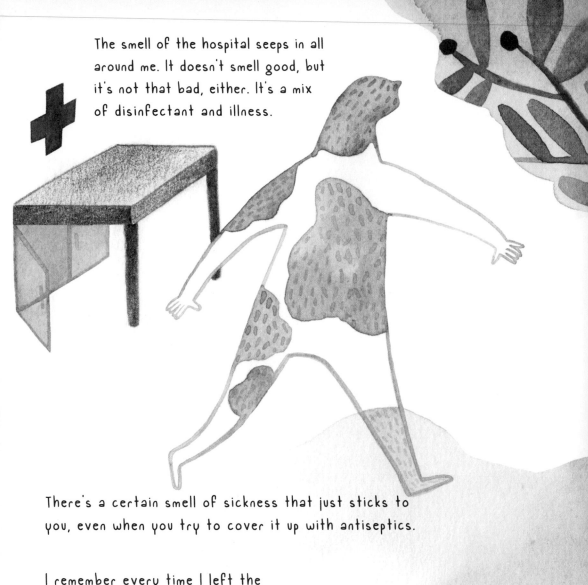

There's a certain smell of sickness that just sticks to you, even when you try to cover it up with antiseptics.

I remember every time I left the hospital to go home, I never wanted to smell that smell again. I wanted to get away from it. I wanted my mum to spray my room with something really nice, like lavender, my favourite scent. Mmmmm!

I wanted to breathe in lavender everywhere... in my bath, on my sheets, on my skin.

I have to say that my parents have been incredibly strong throughout all of this.

And I know I haven't always been easy on my mum, these past years.

It's just that there are some things that I really didn't want her to say to me. I didn't want her to tell me that I was strong.

Or that I was going to survive this struggle.

The problem is... people look at you in a certain way when
you have cancer. It's a look that says you're going to die.
You can see it in their eyes and it's terrifying!

I just wanted everyone to treat me like a normal person. Not feel sorry for me, or tell me how strong I was, or that I could beat this disease.

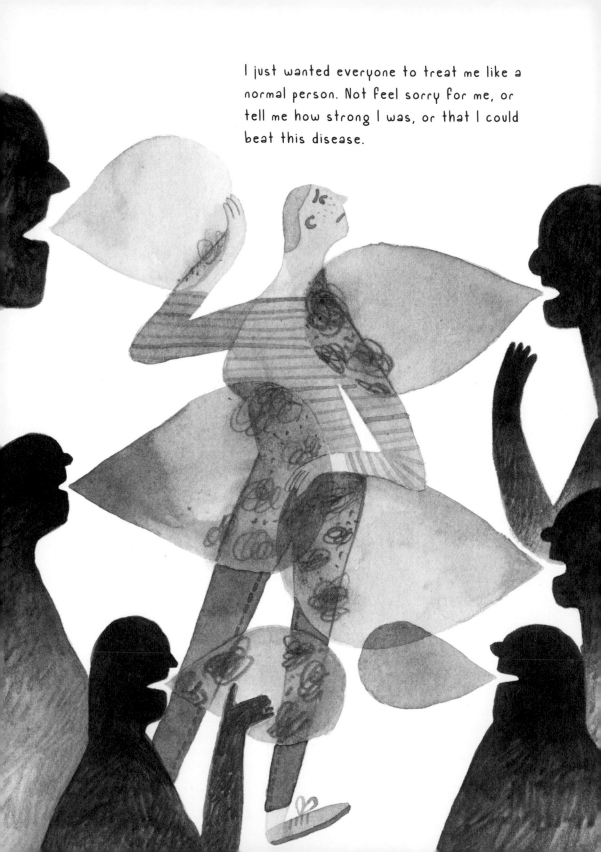

I never pictured what I was going through as a battle anyway because there was nothing I could do to fight it. All I could do was let everything happen to me and try not to complain too much. I know everybody was just trying to help me. In the end, I got used to hearing all those words of encouragement that we say to people when we think we're reassuring them.

Anyway, what can you say to someone who's probably going to die?

I shared a room with Maxine, but she died last
year... and definitely not because she wasn't
strong enough or didn't fight hard enough.

Maxine was the most positive person I've ever
known. She was the kind of person who would
make flowers out of tissues and give them
to the nurses who were taking care of us.
Everybody loved her! She taught me how to
make them too.

It gave us something to do when we had too
much of a headache after our treatments to
watch TV or play video games.

One day, a little while after Maxine died, my mother told me for the hundredth time how strong I was, that she had so much confidence in me, and that she knew I'd get well... even though I'd told her so many times not to say that. So I decided to ask her the question that I'd been too afraid to ask before.

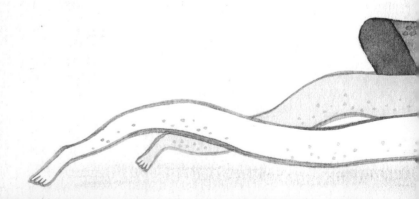

Mum, if I don't get better, will you be disappointed in me?

Right away, she replied,
Of course not, sweetie!

I think she finally understood what I
was trying to tell her because she
never said that to me again.

I could get used to other people saying things like that to me, but not my mum. She had to be able to accept, just like I did, that I might not be able to recover from this disease. And that it wasn't my fault.

I was really hard on my mum. Every time I went in for treatment, she did all she could so it wouldn't feel like a hospital room. She decorated the room with posters, but I finally had to tell her that I was over that boy band because it was so embarrassing in front of the other kids in my room. She would bring stuffed animals, my sister's drawings and balloons.

I think she felt the same way I did about the hospital's interior design!

My dad always tried to keep things light by making jokes.
He embarrassed me so many times with his wisecracks!

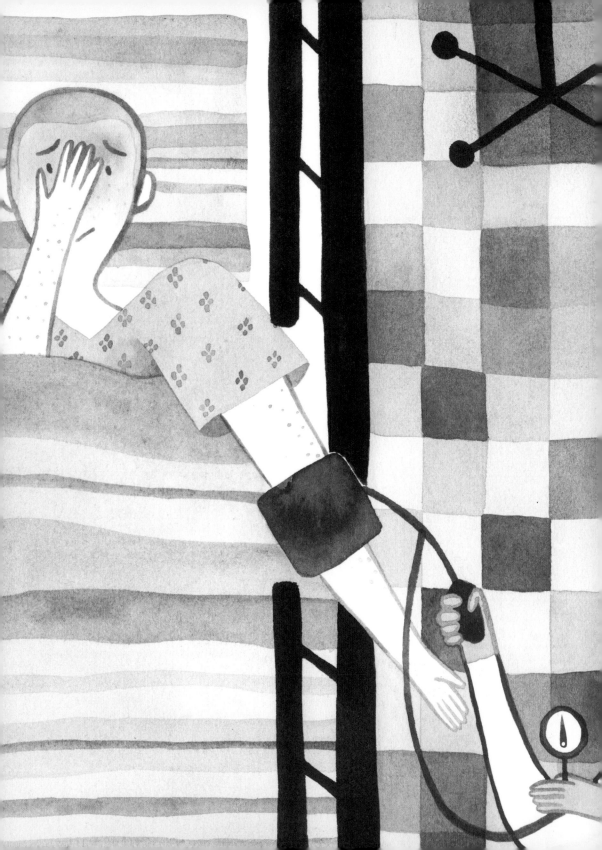

I really hated it when he would say crazy things to the nurse if she came in to take my temperature or my blood pressure when he was there.

I don't know why he always did that. Just to be friendly? So people would think he was cool?

Once, after he cracked one of his
typical, corny jokes to a nurse who
had just given me a shot of morphine,
I asked him why he did that.

I don't remember what he said
because I was really weak, but I know
he reached out and held my hand, and
I saw tears in his eyes.

Maybe I'm confused with another time, but it's the only memory I have of him being so emotional. After that, I decided not to insult him any more about his sense of humour.

I realised that it was a kind of shell that he had for protection, and that I should probably find one for myself too.

My parents and I are
walking down the hospital
corridor now, heading
towards the results we've
been waiting for for
so long. We know that
whatever the answer, we're
completely powerless.

My sister didn't come with us today because she had school.
She made quite a scene this morning because she really
wanted to come. She said she wouldn't be able to concentrate
on school anyway because she couldn't stop thinking about it.

My parents finally promised to call her at school as soon as
we found out. She wasn't happy about it, but they insisted.

Sometimes I feel guilty about my sister. I get a lot more attention from my parents because I'm sick, and she's had to stay with my grandparents a lot.

I really don't like some of the thoughts
that come into my head, either. Like, that
everybody would just be better off if I died.

I even said that to my mum once when we were having a big fight. I know it really hurt her feelings. I apologised right away and we forgave each other, but it didn't stop me from thinking it.

I talked about it to Annie. I used to tell her everything while she was taking my blood tests so I wouldn't think about what she was doing. I really hate needles! She told me...

If you died, they wouldn't be as relieved as they would if you got better.

I know it's really hard, but you just have to stay positive.

I'd be lying if I said
that I could actually
do that. Sometimes
you lose hope.
Sometimes you even
want to die so the
pain will go away.

But you can't say it out
loud. It would just hurt
everyone too much.

Maxine knew, though.
Some nights, we would
talk about what it
would be like to die.
Maxine thought it
would be a whole new
life with no sickness,
and she could start all
over again.

It wasn't so clear for
me. I imagined myself
haunting my friends
and family.

Especially Victor.

About three years ago, a girl
from my school had a party and I
decided to go.

I got really tired and I was just
about to leave because my social
skills were failing me, when
Victor came over.

He twirled his fingers around one of
the ends of the knot in my bandana
that was hanging down my neck,
and said,
Your scarf's cute.

I answered,
It's not a fashion statement. It's because I have cancer.

I was really sorry that I reacted that way just when I was finally
being treated like a normal person. For once, someone was looking
at me like an ordinary girl and not someone sick. I never ever saw
death in Victor's eyes. He looked down at the ground and whispered,

Sorry.
I told him that I was sorry too, and I
thanked him for liking my bandana.

He smiled. After that, we became friends.

And then one day, I was at the hospital for a routine
check up, and Annie asked me if I had any new symptoms
or was having any other health issues so she could
note it in my file for the doctor.

I told her that I'd been feeling a bit nauseous and kind of dizzy lately. She wanted to know more and asked me, All the time?
I told her that I almost always felt that way when I was with Victor. And that I was kind of wondering if I was becoming used to people feeling sorry for me and, since Victor never did that, maybe I was having psychosomatic symptoms to get more of his attention.

vertigo ✓
nausea ✓
fever ✓
in love

Annie burst out laughing and crossed out the notes she had just written. Then, she turned to me and whispered,

It sounds to me like you're in love.

That was when Maxine was still alive. We used to talk about Victor all the time. When Annie was on duty, she would let us stay up, but the other nurses always came in and told us to go to sleep.

We never listened to them though. We just kept on whispering to each other.

I really miss Maxine.
It just feels so empty
here without her, and
inside me too. Maxine
was my best friend.

We had a lot more in common than
just our illness. We thought about
things in the same way.

When Maxine died, my mum gave me
a locket with her picture in it, and
I always keep it on me so she's still
there to bring me good luck.

I give my name to the receptionist and she tells us to sit down in the waiting room. On pink and green benches that are really uncomfortable. And pretty ugly, too.

Of course, my dad has to make one of his silly jokes. I roll my eyes at him before we even sit down.

I can hear the same hospital sounds all around us. There's always noise in the hospital... a telephone rings, a trolley goes rolling by, water running, people talking, an intercom calling out for someone. At first, all those sounds really bothered me and I couldn't sleep.

I got used to it though, and now they kind of reassure me. They used to keep me company when I was feeling so alone. Sometimes I even try to remember them at home because they seem to help me fall asleep.

Victor is texting me. We've been going out for two years now.
It took a long time before I was able to relax and let myself go.
I didn't think I would ever be able to feel such strong emotions.
Being in love almost made me feel nauseous, like after my treatments.
It was too intense. I think I was really afraid of so many things.
Especially, losing Victor.

Once, I got sick at school and Victor came with me to the hospital.

I was really embarrassed because I didn't want him to see me like that. We laugh about it now because he tells everybody (except my parents, of course) that the first time he ever saw my bum was through the crack of a hospital nightgown!

That makes me laugh. I think he's still bragging about it.

We're still waiting for the doctor to call us. I tell myself that if I'm going to die, at least I'll know what it means to be in love. Thanks to Victor. I'd like to text that to him but he really doesn't like it when I say things like that. He gets kind of mad at me. Anyway, my dad is giving me the look because he doesn't think I should be using my mobile phone here.

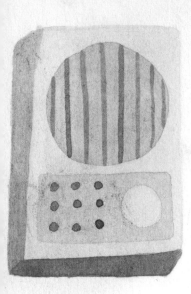

The sound of the intercom
startles me when I hear them
call my name, as if I'd just been
caught using my mobile when
I shouldn't be.

My parents gather their things
and we head over to the
doctor's office.

I've got butterflies in my stomach, but this time it's not because I'm in love. I'm really scared. I touch my locket for luck and think of Maxine.

I think about everything I'll miss if they tell me I'm going
to die... my mum, my dad, my sister, cookies, TV shows I'll
never get to see the end of, dinosaur gummy bears that
are kind of sour, but not too sour, my history class,
walking outside when it's really nice, the smell of autumn,
the starry sky on a full moon, my grandparents, my
grandpa's lasagna, kissing Victor, Victor's eyes, Victor's
voice, Victor's smell, Victor's hands... Victor.

At least the doctor doesn't make us wait too long
before she gives us the news. It's always better to
rip a bandage off fast. People who do it slowly must
really like pain. Any doctor that's about to give you
your life sentence doesn't want to torture you with it.

I asked my mum not to cry, whatever happens, but she breaks down in tears anyway and holds me tight. My dad gives me three little taps on the shoulder but I know he'll have a lot more to say later on. He just can't express himself right now. Anyway, it's better that we don't all lose it right there in front of the doctor.

Our hearts lighten as we leave the hospital. Finally,
we know what's going to happen! Victor is waiting
outside. Right away, my parents ask him,

Why aren't you in school?

He just ignores them, and even though I would like to ask
the same thing, I don't. Instead, I run straight towards
him. I'm so happy to see him, no matter how he got here!
I jump into his arms and I can't hold back the tears.

He pushes me away so he can look into my eyes, and says,
I'm ready. Tell me everything. I want you to know that I'll be
there until the end, even if you don't want me to be.

I'm all smiles, my voice trembling and my throat choked with emotion, as I tell him what we just found out a few minutes ago.

I'm cured!

He wouldn't want me to tell you that he cried, so
I won't, but I can tell you that we didn't let go of
each other for a very long time.

I'm fifteen years old, and they just
told me today that I'm going to live.

About the Story

A few years ago, best-selling author India Desjardins was on a visit to a hospital in Montreal, Québec. There, she met a 10-year-old girl with leukaemia. The girl told her that she was fed up. All the stories about children like her who had cancer had sad endings, so she didn't want to read them. She asked India to write a story about cancer with a happy ending instead, one with laughter and romance.

India did. At first, it was published on the internet, as she wanted the girl to read it as soon as possible. However, the girl was too scared. She was terrified that the story would have a sad ending, like all of the others.

Some years later, the story was turned into a book and the girl finally read it. Even though India hadn't known whether she would recover while she was writing, many of the things she wrote turned out to be true for the girl too. Like the girl in the story, she was now cured. Also, during her illness, she had fallen in love.

Today, around eight out of ten children who are diagnosed with cancer are cured. This story was written to give any child who has cancer hope.

For Emma. For hope. ID

Brimming with creative inspiration, how-to projects, and useful information to enrich your everyday life, Quarto Knows is a favourite destination for those pursuing their interests and passions. Visit our site and dig deeper with our books into your area of interest: Quarto Creates, Quarto Cooks, Quarto Homes, Quarto Lives, Quarto Drives, Quarto Explores, Quarto Gifts, or Quarto Kids.